Shining a Light on
THE MUELLER REPORT

A Readable Version for Everyone

JOYCE SILVER

Print information available on the last page

Rev. date: 07/09/2019

To order additional copies of this book, contact:
Xlibris
1-888-795-4274
www.Xlibris.com
Orders@Xlibris.com

Shining a Light on
THE MUELLER REPORT

A Readable Version for Everyone

JOYCE SILVER

Table Of Contents

4   ACKNOWLEDGEMENTS

5   INTRODUCTION

6   Preamble

8   MUELLER REPORT VOLUME 1

20   Financial Times article: Trump's Russian Connection by Michael Stott & Catherine Belton, 12/13/2016

28   MUELLER REPORT, VOLUME 2

45   Editorial by Joyce Silver

48   GLOSSARY

ACKNOWLEDGEMENTS

First, I'd like to acknowledge and thank my son, Edward, for his unceasing commitment to our relationship and his love! We've travelled many roads together and he's the person I know I can call in any emergency. Much love & thank you Edward. Our journey together continues. Next, I'd like to thank my 3 grandchildren for their constant love and support. Though, I have baked with Irina, I'm there for all of them with unconditional love, support and intellectual stimulation. Thank you, Irina, Issac & Eilon for your constant love, as well.

I especially would like to thank my dear friend and editor, Kathaleen Grant, for her ceaseless dedication to my writing excellence, her skills, editorial advice and perseverance while working with me. More than that, because we have a shared vision of our Country and a real dedication to activism and service, we worked together to create an extraordinary book. I can't thank her enough for undertaking this project with me. As Kathaleen stated, she would not have committed to work with anyone else. I'm deeply flattered that she values me and our work together.

I'd like to acknowledge the talents of my good friend, Justin Weingartner, for his political cartoons, that have appeared on my Word Press Blog Posts, and thank him for his constant support and friendship, as well.

My friends Meryl Rubin, Mary Lou Steiner, Yvette Bendahan, Alice Shields, Edgar Osorio, Wray Gunn & Cora Portnoff, Chad & Fran Debordeau, Adriana Weiss, my surrogate granddaughter, Pat Sills, Barbara Sims and everyone at the Stephen Wise Free Synagogue and my monthly book club. You've all befriended me, nurtured and supported me.

In addition, I would like to thank my "old" friends, Joel and Evelyn Harris, who led me to Xlibris. Many thanks to the professional staff at XLibris especially, Carlos Cortez, Grey Edwards, and Renee Ashton, who made publication of this book possible on a timely basis.

Last but not least, I'd like to acknowledge and thank the many people in my life, too numerous to name, whom I might not have acknowledged at this time, but hold in high esteem. Thank you everyone. I've crossed so many people's paths and I have been lucky to come away with new friends who have supported and befriended me on my Journey. At last, I'm an Author. My parents would have been proud.

INTRODUCTION

I truly care about the preservation of our Democracy and the State of our Union. That's why, I chose to write this synopsis of the Mueller Report.

Once Robert Mueller published his report, I had to read it, to understand the facts behind The Russian Intervention in our 2016 Elections. Reading the Mueller Report, consumed a grueling eight hours a day for a solid week. Reverting to my graduate school days, I took meticulous notes, reading Mueller's facts behind Russia's Interference in our 2016 Elections and their cooperative efforts with Candidate Trump, effectively elevating him to the Presidency. Now, as I have always done throughout my career, I sought to understand why a future President of these United States would accept a foreign power's help without question. I remain stunned.

I read the Mueller Report in its entirety. It stirred feelings within me of both patriotism and a strong desire to create a document for everyone to read and understand easily. I crafted a synopsis based on my notes and I sincerely hope that you will feel like I did after reading this version of the Mueller Report: we must pursue Justice to preserve our Democracy.

"We the People" are entitled to know all the facts about Trump's Russian connections that are detailed in Mueller's Report, Volume 1. Volume 2 provides the roadmap for Obstruction of Justice by listing the many instances of obstruction by the President during his Administration, linking those instances to incidents that took place in Volume 1.

Finally, on my Editorial page, I have provided my own thoughts as a result of this very intense experience. I passionately believe Congress should begin the process of Impeachment *immediately* based on the Obstruction of Justice facts laid out in Mueller's Report, Volume 2. This action, in turn, would allow Congress and the American People to see the entire Mueller Report. It would negate Attorney Client privilege and assure that all witnesses called would provide truthful commentary or legally be held in contempt. Once the case for Obstruction of Justice proceeds pending Impeachment, the House of Representatives becomes a coequal branch of Government with independent rights.

Then and only then will we have the whole picture of what went on, and I believe that all the American People will then support Impeachment of this President, without a doubt!

Very Truly Yours,
Joyce Silver

Preamble

Herein lies the basis for the Obstruction of Justice Case, based on the definition of Obstruction of Justice, as defined by the 2002 Congress and supported by Justice Antonin Scalia. President Donald Trump's actions merit obstruction charges, pending impeachment.

"We the People" are confronted with Trump, his family and others in the Campaign, waiting for the GRU (Russia's Military Intelligence Service) to release the stolen John Podesta & DNC (Democratic National Committee) emails to WikiLeaks, who then would release them to the Country. On 7/14/16, WikiLeaks confirmed it received the encrypted stolen emails from the GRU. It alerted the team, who were waiting anxiously for their release, all 20,000 of them, three days before the DNC Convention. This release of tranches of emails was intended to cause maximum harm to the DNC, showing a Party purported to be divided.

"We the People" should understand the magnitude of this theft of property. How is this different from physically breaking into a locked DNC headquarters, as in Watergate? Trump, his family and the Campaign were not physically doing the burglary. How it occurred is redacted, but we do know the burglary was anticipated and they were waiting for the successful results of the efforts of the GRU & Wikileaks, and they were rewarded.

Fifty thousand emails between Podesta and Hillary Clinton, the Clinton Foundation, her Campaign, and her private speeches the preceding year were released. All the emails came from Podesta's private email account, but how they were taken is redacted by William Barr, the Attorney General.

On 7/27/16, Trump goes on national TV and states, "Russia, if you're listening, I hope you're able to find Clinton's 30,000 missing emails." He is referring to the emails on Clinton's server when she was Secretary of State. The GRU methodology was redacted. Ultimately, the GRU stole 300 gigabytes of data from the DNC's cloud-based account and releases them. After only 47 pages into the Mueller Report, we are hit with the enormity of this theft of the DNC emails: Clinton's personal and public data, Podesta's emails, and a Clinton aide's emails. A foreign government has hacked the emails of Candidate Trump's rival, at his command, in order to benefit Trump, his family, and members of his Campaign Team.

Certainly, "We the People" now know that the release of these emails had occurred and others were the subject of discussion at the June 9th meeting in Trump Tower. Trump intended to get "dirt" on Clinton, his opponent; he was rewarded by the Russians, and he used that dirt to smear "dirty Hillary" for all to see.

If the tie back to Trump were not true, why did and does Trump still attempt to obstruct justice? Why is Barr spinning falsehoods and obstructing justice? Why did Sessions lie to Congress about his Russian connections? They all lied for 2 1/2 years to cover up a blatant crime that has been committed against the other political party, as well as the People of the United States.

This most surely had to have been agreed to in advance; the cooperation with a Foreign Power was too extraordinary to be coincidental. "We the People" must be concerned that all our data is too vulnerable to foreign countries seeking to divide our Nation and destroy our faith in the System and the Rule of Law. What Laws will protect our vote from future Foreign Country interventions in our Elections?

Worse, Russia targeted our voting machines, as well as State Boards of Elections, Secretaries of State, counties and individuals associated with these entities. We must ask ourselves, are we more secure today from cyber attacks than we were in 2016? If not, why not?

The facts speak for themselves. Even with redactions, our voting systems and our political elections process have been compromised by Russia. Furthermore, Russian money and Russian individuals, organized ad campaigns and rallies on behalf of the Trump Campaign and aggressively targeted the Democratic Party and Hillary Clinton. Russia, Trump and WikiLeaks impugned Hilary Clinton's character. Some will counter and say that the US is capable of skewing foreign elections, too. This is true. However, if you're going to use "back channels" to destroy America's opponents, we should be smart enough to make sure no Americans and no American systems are equally vulnerable. Where is or was American superiority when massive cybersecurity was needed and is required?

Why aren't all Americans enraged over our system failures? Why aren't the American people appalled by the unethical and immoral behavior of this President, his family, his Campaign and Transition teams?

If we want Justice to be done, we must demand an inquiry into Obstruction of Justice, pending Impeachment. That is the only way to know the truth. The American People are entitled to the unredacted work product of The Special Counsel. Let us all read about the magnitude of Russian Interference in our Election and further understand why Trump and his team accepted Russia's help. It appears that when winning is everything and there are no rules of engagement, it is up to "We the People" to demand equal Justice. We have been wronged and we continue to be wronged. We are paying for current Republican Party Policy with our lives.

MUELLER REPORT VOLUME 1

There is nothing in the Mueller Report that condones Trump's actions or the actions of his children and his inner circle of associates. The Mueller Report, Volume 1, details how Donald Trump, his children and friends worked side by side with the Russians as they passed stolen property to them via the WikiLeaks conduit. The Russian GRU helped TRUMP win the Presidency at great cost to "We the People" with a potential payout to the Trump Organization in the billions. How did the Russians specifically help Trump? Read on!

1. Both the GRU & WikiLeaks encrypted their internal communications to the Trump organization. Since they were aiding Trump, his campaign and family, WikiLeaks would inform them when to expect the stolen data, how to de-encrypt the data, and how to retweet the contents of the stolen data. P43

2. The stolen DNC & Podesta emails were transferred from the GRU, using the Internet Research Agency, to WikiLeaks. The *how* is redacted.

3. On 7/14/16, The GRU sent an encrypted document to WikiLeaks via the Ecuadorian Embassy. WikiLeaks confirmed receipt and the ability to open the documents, containing 20,000 emails from the DNC. The DNC Convention convened 3 days later, after the stolen documents were released to the Public. Page 46

   • Dear readers, we might ask was this legal? Unlike breaking and entering a building and physically stealing documents, there is no Law delineating theft of private property by computers, domestic or foreign or monetizing that theft. Congress and the Courts have never codified computer theft of private property, though you could make a case for copies of the emails and DNC strategies, being subject to case law, it is not a 100% known method to proceed.

4. During this entire section, discussing the passing off of documents between the GRU and WikiLeaks, whole paragraphs are redacted, citing "Investigative Technique". Fifty thousand emails were released in all between Podesta and Clinton, the Clinton Campaign and Foundation, including Clinton's private speeches given on 10/7 & 11/7. All the emails came from Podesta's private email account, the latest one, dated 5/21/16, was released purposely to coincide with the Democratic National Convention as the Trump Campaign tried to cast doubts on Hillary Clinton's" electability".

5. Additional GRU cyber operations targeted Democratic linked targets in the Summer & Fall Of 2016. On 7/27/16, Trump went on TV requesting that: "Russia if you're listening, I hope you're able to find the 30,000 emails that are missing?" These were the 30,000 emails stored on Clinton's server while serving as Secretary of State. Some emails belonged to a Clinton aide. It's not clear how the GRU found and identified these email accounts, as that was never made public. We do know that Russian efforts to retrieve these emails were motivated by Trump's National televised plea for their release.

   • Then as we continue to read the Mueller Report, there are more redactions on GRU methodology. Why?

   • The Mueller Report concluded that the GRU was able to take a snapshot of a snapshot of databases that were producing backups. P49: Why is Mueller's investigative technique obscured, or the DNC's cloud computing service redacted?

   • Who is being protected?

6. The GRU stole approximately 300 gigabytes of data from the DNC cloud-based account. Shouldn't "We the People" demand to know which service was used and if it is *now* secure?

7. **Mueller Report heading: <u>Intrusions Targeting the Administration of US Elections</u>** GRU (Russia's Intelligence Service) officers targeted individuals and entities, such as the State Boards of Election, Secretaries of State, county governments and individuals connected to these agencies.

8. Mueller did not investigate the hacking of our voting machines in all 50 States, nor did he follow up on the reason to compromise the voter rolls in Illinois and counties in Florida. I can only assume these databases became the targets of a customized Social Media campaign designed to damage Hillary Clinton and Bernie Sanders.

9. The attack on our Election process and the Russian use of our voter registration rolls were left to the FBI, Homeland Security and the States to investigate.

   • There is no doubt that Russian interference in our Elections occurred. All investigative reports should be made public. We should all want to know if the integrity of our voting system is being maintained. If not, why not?

- The GRU gained access to voter databases and millions of voter records in Illinois. Was this the polling data given to Konstantin Kilimnik by Michael Flynn? Or were the data transferred from Jeff Sessions to Sergey Kislyak?

- With access to registered voters in Battleground States in the summer of 2016, it would be possible to target these same voters through Social Media. We have been skillfully manipulated! Is it any wonder that Americans are divided?

- Once again, how Russia accomplished these breaches is redacted! **Why?** Every State should be concerned and interested in preventing Russian intrusion again in 2020!

- The Russians also went on phishing expeditions at a voting technology company, in use in States during the 2016 Election, their Corporate name is redacted? **Why?**

- An unnamed county government in Florida was penetrated by the GRU. The FBI investigated. We don't know the outcome or their recommendations? They're redacted. **Why?**

- On P51, entire chapters on "Trump Campaign and the dissemination of hacked materials" and "Contacts with the Campaign about WikiLeaks" were redacted. **Why?**

- By P53, according to Rick Gates, by the late summer of 2016, The Trump Campaign was planning a press conference, a communications campaign and messaging based on the possible release of the Clinton emails by WikiLeaks. They're on their way to LaGuardia when a call comes in for Trump. Who is redacted, due to Harm to ongoing matter? Then, Trump told Gates that more releases of damaging information would be coming. (Almost the entire P53 is redacted, along with redactions through pages 57.)

- By September 2016, Jerome Corsi and Ted Malloch knew that John Podesta's emails were coming and assured the Trump campaign that they would be in the driver's seat. The rest of p56 and 58 are redacted, presumably not to harm Trump. What is this material about?

10. Donald Trump Jr had direct access to WikiLeaks during the campaign period. In his communication with WikiLeaks, it appears Julian Assange is concerned that Clinton would send a drone to kill him. In retaliation, he sends Trump Jr a message on how to share information with his Dad that would help Trump to look through the Podesta emails. *Two days later, Trump Jr publicly tweeted the WikiLeaks link, as a thank you! P60*

11. Prior to WikiLeaks getting the Clinton deleted emails from Russia, there was a phishing expedition started by Michael Flynn. He was asked by Trump, to obtain the emails anyway possible, including using the services of the Chinese, Russian and Iranians.

12. **"Campaign efforts to obtain deleted Clinton emails"** P 62

    ✓ Clinton's unprotected server was in the process of being hacked by State related players and private mercenaries.

    ✓ Sam Clovis, the Campaign co-chair for Trump, was in the loop, along with Flynn, Steve Bannon, Kellyanne Conway, Edward Prince (Betsy DeVos' brother) and Peter Smith. Far from a group of bungling idiots, these folks were intensely serious about their pursuit of the Clinton emails from any possible source.

13. Regarding Russian Government links to and contacts with the Trump Campaign, it appears that Mueller was looking for a quid pro quo, established between Trump and/or the Campaign and the GRU. However, during a 30-year relationship with Russia, a quid pro quo could have been established at any time.

14. The Financial Times article, dated 12/13/16, included in this Pamphlet, details Trump's relationship with the Russians. His ties to the Ukraine and Georgia go back 30 years, along with his relationships with Paul Manafort, Flynn and others in his inner circle.

    • When was a quid pro quo established? Does it matter? Trump coordinated seamlessly with WikiLeaks and the GRU.

    • Furthermore, Russia, a foreign power, paid for his rallies, targeted his voters and cost him only $70 Million to follow the information left for his campaign to follow by WikiLeaks. ***Is this legal? Absolutely Not!***

15. Russia set the scene and Trump played his part. By 2/14 a letter of Intent had been signed between Trump Jr representing the Trump Organization and the Crocus Group, headed by the Real Estate developer, Aras Agalarov. All this occurred after Trump's trip to Moscow for the Miss Universe contest. This deal never moved forward, until 2016.

16. When it was clear that Trump would become the Republican nominee in 2016, Trump Jr and Ivanka Trump, went back to Russia to sign a better deal with the same group, codified by a Letter of Intent, on Trump's behalf.

17. Discussion of the Trump Tower project proceeds again from 2015-16, with Trump Jr, Ivanka Trump, Michael Cohen, Felix Sater & Rozov. A Letter of Intent is signed. Two persons before the Grand Jury are redacted. I assume Trump Jr & Ivanka Trump are the persons of interest to the Grand Jury. Further information on P 69 places them both in Moscow looking for deals in the mid 2000's.

18. Meanwhile, Michael Cohen continues to update Trump on the project's progress. More Russians come into the mix and they want to set up meetings with Trump at the highest level of the Russian Government. One of the Russians had worked with Trump previously on a building project in Batumi, Georgia in 2011. Following their signing of Letters of Intent in 2015, Sater contacts Cohen, stating that together with him, Sater would get to Putin's team and "they will make sure Donald Trump is President."

19. There is a follow up letter, as Sater envisions Trump and Putin cutting the Trump Moscow "ribbon" in an opening ceremony for Trump's commercial real estate venture. "Putin wants to deal with a pragmatic leader and a successful businessman. Business, politics, whatever, it's all the same for everyone who knows how to deal".

20. The money to be made by Trump would exceed $1Billion with no risk. A kingly sum, indeed! Trump looked upon his campaign as a significant "infomercial" for Trump branded properties P 71-72.

21. On 11/16/15, Ivanka Trump received an email from a Russian stating her husband ran Putin's campaign and would help her father (Trump). Either, Lana Alexander, or Ivanka is redacted by Barr. The Grand Jury information is also redacted. The story gets increasingly complicated on 7/27/18, when an email to Mueller from Arcova Development states they were promising Trump "land in the Crimea plus an informal visit with Vladimir Putin," etc.

    • Though the Real Estate project lay idle, Trump was still pursuing The Trump Tower Moscow project through mid-Campaign 2016, when a Letter of Intent was signed by Trump Jr and Ivanka.

22. The Real Estate development project proceeded with a "flourish of activity and pauses". Many players are brought into the mix, and finally in December 2015, VTB Bank got involved and informal "business" meetings were proposed with Putin.

23. Cohen's and Trump's passports were issued Visas to Moscow with a celebration planned at the Russian Consulate.

24. Meanwhile, Felix Sater involved a third party, redacted due to proceedings before the Grand Jury, with ties to Genbank in Crimea, Ukraine.

25. The US government had sanctions out on this man (redacted) and he has been deported from the USA.

26. Cohen intended to go to Moscow before the Cleveland RNC Convention and Trump was to go to Moscow afterward. P76

27. Nothing more seems to happen on the Real Estate Development Project. However, the plot to deal with Putin continued and more people enter and exit. They all have one thing in common, an overwhelming ambition to do business with the Kremlin and/or to show they have foreign policy expertise.

28. On page 84 we come to another redaction. It appears that Barr wants to shield Trump, because he's backing away from NATO & taking a weaker stance on Russian aggression in the Ukraine.

29. A foreign policy team is being assembled. Trump was approached by George Papadopoulos, asking if Trump would consider a possible meeting with Putin. Trump and Sessions were interested.

30. It appears, based on all the players and all the convoluted evidence, when Trump finally asks Russia, in a tweet to help his campaign and release the Clinton emails, Trump knew they existed.

31. Papadopoulos, a member of the foreign policy team, also knew individuals associated with the Internet Research Agency (GRU). The Russians provided all the information to WikiLeaks, who dumped Clinton's emails, when the time was right, to hurt her chances for the Presidential Election.

32. It appears, all the redactions on these pages, may be shielding President Trump! On P 85, as we continue reading the Mueller Report, many people think they were bringing Trump and Putin together for a common purpose. Papadopoulos communicated with Stephen Miller & Corey Lewandowski on 4/25/16, stating that he can get the Clinton emails, and Putin is ready to meet with Trump on neutral territory. (Note: The meeting, to our knowledge, did not take place until after Trump's inauguration, when Trump met with Putin in Helsinki.)

33. Based on this "new" information, a foreign adversary approached the US Government, on 7/26/16, a few days after the release of one tranche of Clinton emails by WikiLeaks, prompting then President Obama to contact the FBI to open an investigation into a possible coordinated effort between the Trump Campaign and Russia.

34. The Trump Campaign management went through internal turmoil during the summer of 2016. Papadopoulos was fired in October 2016 for making comments to a Russian news agency.

35. P 93 is redacted, and new people were introduced to the Grand Jury, probably Sam Clovis, Miller or Lewandowski. They all have "amnesia" on Papadopoulos' messages from Putin and the GRU.

36. I've read 100 pages into the question of conspiracy with Russia. I understand why the Mueller team was frustrated. So many sources, so many people privy to information about the GRU and Russian intervention in our Election, their coordination with WikiLeaks, and yet there was "no smoking gun" to target. These notes concluded on p 94.

<u>The subsequent pages deal with the following players:</u>

1. Next came Carter Page. Page had worked with the Russians and was accepted onto the Campaign as a Foreign Policy expert, pro-Russian. Though it was never established that Page worked for Russia, the redactions appear to shield individuals of interest. Who are they? Russians? P96.

    o Page was anxious to get back in Russia's Political orbit and billed himself as a man of access and knowledge on Energy. He was honored to speak at the New Economic School in Moscow on 7/16. Page praised Russia and denigrated US Foreign Policy toward Russia and the Russian Sanctions.

    o As a representative of a potential President, he offers Policy in conflict with a sitting President! Page's contacts or dealings with Russia's energy sector are redacted under the heading "Grand Jury", along with his emails to members of Trump's Campaign. Who is being protected and Why?

    o When public scrutiny of Page's contacts and policy became unpopular, he was let go and became unwelcome to the transition team. P101

2. Other interesting Russians are mentioned, including a think tank, CNI, founded by Richard Nixon. AG Sessions was a member of the CNI. Their platform was Strategic Realism in US Foreign Policy.

   o Membership in CNI provided unlimited access to Russian government officials. Jared Kushner attended a CNI event looking for Foreign Policy experts, attacking Hillary Clinton, and promoting a pro-Russian Policy.

   o CNI crafted Trump's speeches and policy, along with Sessions and his aide, Dick Dearborn.

   o On 3/24/16, Kushner puts Simes (Russian born, emigrated to the US in the 1970's) in touch with Stephen Miller, Trump's Sr Policy advisor.

   o Kislyak talks to Trump, Kushner and Sessions, commending them on their stance toward Russia.

3. Kushner & Simes decide to minimize their associations with Russia and instead try to smear Hillary Clinton by showing that she had hidden Russian contacts, thus taking the spotlight off Trump.

   o Deflection is one of many strategies used.

4. On June 9th, 2016 the meeting in the Trump Tower with a Russian prosecutor takes place. The discussion centered on the Magnitsky Act, Sanctions and Hillary Clinton's emails.

   o After these events, the Grand Jury convenes to look at all the players; there were seven at the meeting and their emails and names are redacted.

   o Redactions continue, shielding persons being investigated by the Grand Jury and their information. P111-112

   o We have gone full circle with the same players from 2013-2014.

5. Trump Jr reappears and gets information from Goldstone stating that Russia's chief prosecutor would provide incriminating evidence on Hillary Clinton. Many people in the Trump Campaign are working in concert to destroy her credibility and her chances to be elected President.

6. On 6/6 and 7, Trump Jr had multiple calls with Agalarov. (heads the Crocus Group that eventually enters into a Letter of Intent in 2016 on Trump Tower Moscow) What transpired at the Trump Tower meeting is the subject of Grand Jury proceedings and redacted on P114.

    o The meeting took place and Trump's children attended. Trump was informed of the meeting that was now scheduled for June 9th, to discuss "dirt" on Hillary, etc.

    o On P117, all Information and Russians associated with the meeting are the subject of the Grand Jury and redacted. The Grand Jury is still empowered.

    o Once an investigation into Impeachment begins, the Truth on what transpired at the Trump Tower meeting and the participants will be revealed. All Grand Jury notes are redacted about Sanctions & the Magnitsky AG Sessions, speaking for Trump, at a conference held by the Heritage Foundation in conjunction with the State Department, stated they were looking for better relations with Russia. 80 Foreign Ambassadors were present, including Kislyak.

    o This event took place during the RNC Convention. Sessions spoke with 6-12 Ambassadors after the speech, and one was Kislyak.

    o The RNC subsequently changed its platform to provide appropriate assistance to the Ukraine, not lethal assistance, based on Trump's request.

    o Mueller's investigative notes are also redacted. P 121

7. Next, Manafort is investigated by Mueller. He was involved with the ex-dictator of Eastern Ukraine looking for a peace deal.

    o Manafort shared polling data with the Russians.

    o Manafort had numerous ties to Russia and Ukraine oligarchs.

    o Barr redacted Mueller's Investigative technique when Mueller is discussing Gates, Kilimnik, Hawker, and Alexander van der zwaan. P134

    o Trump's relationship with Manafort goes back to 1988 when Manafort was given VIP status at the Republican Convention by Trump.

    o Why did Manafort lie? He always protects his business interests. He looked upon his association with Trump as a way to continue monetizing his relationships. The

Grand Jury information is redacted when the information concerns Russians, in this instance, probably Oleg Deripaska. It was purported that Manafort owed Millions to him.

- In January of 2019, Sanctions were lifted on Oleg Deripaska and it's been reported that he is going to build an Aluminum Plant in Kentucky. (Mitch McConnel's home state)

- Manafort became part of the inner Russian circle, speaking in code, talking about the future of Russia. Redacted on p138. Why?

- Redacted information before the Grand Jury may refer to the ex-Ukrainian President? The Report continues through the Summer events of 2016. Manafort's contacts become important to Trump.

- Manafort discussed the Battleground States - Michigan, Wisconsin, Pennsylvania and Minnesota - with Kilimnik, a Russian spy, in August 2016. They also discussed an Eastern Ukraine peace plan. All this is redacted Grand Jury and Investigative Technique commentary.

8. New testimony is introduced and the Grand Jury testimony is redacted around various Russian Sovereign Fund persons and the UAE. Putin wanted greater representation in the Gulf. P148

9. A whole section on Russia's spin on Clinton's loss is redacted under Investigative Technique and Grand Jury Investigation. P149-150

- Putin wants, through intermediaries, to meet Kushner and Trump Jr.

10. Erik Prince becomes a player and we are introduced to other connections with Russia and the UAE, through Prince's contact with George Nader and Kirill Dmitriev.

- Nader tells Prince of Putin's interest in the Trump Administration and all Grand Jury information is redacted.

- Prince brings Steven Mnuchin, Wilbur Ross and Kellyanne Conway into his confidence at a Trump Tower meeting, bringing them up to speed on Dmitriev and Russia's interest in the Trump Administration on 1/3/17.

o Prince is sent to the Seychelles to meet with Nader and Dmitriev. The Grand Jury information is redacted. They assume Steve Bannon sent Prince. Prince told everyone assembled in the Seychelles that Bannon was receptive to detente.

o Prince denies he said anything to Dmitriev.

11. I assume, the Grand Jury must prove that Prince has committed perjury. What is interesting is that by 1/28/17, many subordinates are trying to bring Trump & Putin together. (Wasn't Putin the first person to whom Trump spoke after the inauguration?) Trump is Player #1! P154

12. When Obama sanctioned Russia for interfering in the 2016 election, Trump's response was get over it!

o Trump and his people were conducting Foreign Policy with Russia, prior to his being sworn in. Wasn't this against the Law?

13. Mueller concluded that the Trump Campaign didn't "collude" with Russia. Although this was due to the current definition of collusion (not a legal term), Mueller never found a smoking gun and knew that conspiracy was difficult to prove. The GRU worked seamlessly with WikiLeaks, Trump, his family and his inner circle. These individuals had access to Russian Oligarchs. Putin had to have blessed all transfers of data and presumably had control over the potential Moscow Tower Deal. There is no sunlight between the players. All we can do is follow Mueller's reasoning, which is redacted, as well as the tweets for clarification. Thus, Mueller concluded, obstruction of Justice is the more logical legal path to pursue, laying out a roadmap for Impeachment. P183

o Why is there a redaction when Mueller is summarizing? This information is germane to our understanding of Mueller's reasoning not to pursue collusion. P174

o Why is Mueller's charging decisions wholly redacted under the heading, "Harm to ongoing matter"? Who is being protected by Barr? (P176 &177 and 178 are wholly redacted, along with Mueller's potential indictment of a person under section 1030)

o P179 is redacted under personal privacy invoked by Barr. Who is Barr protecting?

14. There was a Violation of the Foreign Agents Act; many were culpable:

o Those formally charged were Manafort, Gates and Flynn. Mueller would have charged others, but the information is redacted, citing personal privacy. Whose privacy is being protected?

15. The Trump Tower meeting in June was cited by Mueller as a Violation of Campaign Finance law and it is redacted.

   o Wasn't everything Putin, Russian citizens and Ukrainians did for and with Trump in violation of our existing Laws?

   o Utilizing Social Media, political rallies, the hacking of voting machines, and the American People's data, isn't it evident that Russia influenced our 2016 election?

   o Was providing hacked emails and correspondence of the DNC, Podesta, and Clinton to the Public in violation of our Laws?

   o Was the GRU/Russian intervention of value to Trump and didn't that violate our Laws?

   o Has anyone fixed our voting machines? Are they still open to cyber attack along with individuals responsible for guaranteeing our vote?

   o The individuals at the June 9 Trump Tower meeting assumed they were above the Law. Were they disingenuously waiting for other shoes to drop while aiding Putin and tabling Sanctions?

   o Mueller's reasoning on Trump's criminal culpability is Redacted. Why? Mueller was discussing his reasoning for not prosecuting Campaign Finance or giving a value to Clinton's emails. P189 is partially Redacted (Harm to Ongoing Matter). What was he getting at, after not charging Trump Jr or Kushner? (Mueller's reasoning is Redacted on P188 and p189.)

16. Next, Mueller considers Constitutional Considerations and those are redacted on p 190 and 191.

17. As part of Mueller's Summary, he refers to Obstruction of Justice to fully understand who is liable for making false statements to a Grand Jury. "We the People " need the information which has been redacted to fully understand the case for or against conspiracy, in Mueller's words. ("We the People" vs Donald Trump.)

18. Volume 1 of the Mueller Report on Collusion ends with many redactions and questions left unanswered. I will provide a Glossary of all individuals and organizations involved.

The Financial Times Article below reviews Donald Trump's relationships with Russians over a 30-year period.

Trump's Russian connections

Donald Trump's ties to Russia are back under the spotlight after the CIA concluded that Moscow had interfered in November's presidential election to help the Republican candidate win

Donald Trump

Donald Trump

TRUMP'S RUSSIA INTEREST SPARKED IN THE SOVIET YEARS

The Republican candidate's links to Russia are a mix of bling, business and bluster spanning 30 years. This account in five sections traces Trump's fascination for Russia from its beginnings in Soviet times through deals done in the Putin era to Trump's appointment of a slew of Russia-connected advisers during the US presidential campaign. It concludes with outside views on Trump's long-standing Russia ties and the president-elect's own explanations.

Yuri Dubinin
A first contact from Moscow

In 1986 Soviet ambassador Yuri Dubinin sat next to Donald Trump at a New York lunch and they talked about Trump Tower. "One thing led to another, and now I'm talking about building a large luxury hotel across the street from the Kremlin in partnership with the Soviet government," the tycoon recalled in his book Trump: The Art of the Deal. Trump flew to Moscow at Dubinin's invitation to discuss the hotel project with the Soviet tourism agency.

Mikhail Gorbachev
No glasnost at Trump Tower

The hotel never materialised but Trump aides promised something even better: Soviet leader Mikhail Gorbachev and his wife, Raisa, would tour Trump Tower during a 1988 visit to New York. Trump said Gorbachev wanted to see the building because "it's become the hottest building in New York". But the visit didn't happen: the Gorbachevs visited other Manhattan landmarks and Trump rushed out of his tower to greet a lookalike of the Soviet leader.

Zurab Tsereteli
Russia's Columbus seeks the new world

Trump's Russia connections continued under Gorbachev's successor, Boris Yeltsin. Trump attempted in 1997 to erect a giant bronze statue of Christopher Columbus donated by the Russian government at his development on the Hudson river. Taller than the Statue of Liberty, the artwork was crafted by Zurab Tsereteli, a close friend of the Moscow mayor. It ended up in Puerto Rico after several US cities refused to accept it.

TRUMP'S RUSSIA DEALS AND LINKS MULTIPLY

As financial headaches cramped Trump's style in the US, the property tycoon's organization stepped up efforts to win Russian business.

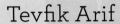

Tevfik Arif
Trump's Russia-connected business partners

By the 2000s, corporate bankruptcies had limited Donald Trump's access to capital markets. An FT investigation showed that the tycoon joined forces with Bayrock, a New York property developer founded by a Soviet-born newcomer to the US, Tevfik Arif, to pursue deals around the world. Their best-known collaboration was Trump SoHo, a 46-storey hotel-condominium completed in 2010.

Ilya Reznik
Coastal Miami becomes little Moscow

Throughout the 2000s, records show Russians were buying millions of dollars of Trump- branded real estate in the US, according to property records reviewed by the FT. The Trump Organization said it did not believe Russians spent more money on Trump ventures than those from other regions. Russian real estate broker Ilya Reznik told the FT that Russian could be heard everywhere in the Trump properties on the Florida coast.

Trump Luxury Vodka
Trump Luxury vodka makes a splash in Moscow

Trump and his partners promoted their "24K Super Premium Vodka", a luxury vodka sold in a bottle decorated with 24-karat gold, at the Millionaire Fair in Moscow in 2007. The fair lured Russian high-spenders with luxury yachts, diamond-encrusted mobile phones and entire islands for sale. The venture later went out of business.

Dmitry Rybolovlev
The oligarch who bought Trump's mansion

Trump's single biggest reported Russian deal to date came in 2008 when fertilizer billionaire Dmitry Rybolovlev purchased the tycoon's Palm Beach mansion for $95m. Trump boasted of the profit he made on the deal, having bought the property four years earlier for only £41m. Trump denied ever meeting the oligarch and said "he just happened to be from Russia".

Eric Trump
Trump's sons promote Russian business

At the same time, the Trump family were gushing with praise for Russians. While marketing Trump SoHo, the tycoon's second son, Eric, told Russian journalists that "the best property buyers are now Russian" while Trump himself said: "I really like Vladimir Putin." Trump's first son, Donald Jr, told eTurboNews that "Russians make up a pretty disproportionate cross-section of a lot of our assets...we see a lot of money pouring in from Russia".

Sergei Millian
The Russian middleman claiming to act for Trump

One of the people who said he brought Russian money into Trump projects was Sergei Millian, head of the Russian-American Chamber of Commerce. His organization said in 2009 it had "signed formal agreements with The Trump Organization" to service Russian real estate clients and Millian bragged about winning Trump's affection at the 2007 Millionaire Fair in Moscow. The Trump Organization denied that Trump had any relationship with him.

Aras Agalarov
Trump's Russian beauty pageant

Moscow property billionaire Aras Agalarov signed a $14m deal to bring Trump's Miss Universe beauty pageant to Moscow in 2013. Trump invited Vladimir Putin, tweeting that the Kremlin chief would be his "new best friend" if he came. The Russian president instead sent a trusted envoy, Kremlin property chief Vladimir Kozhin and a "beautiful present". At the show, Agalarov claimed he had a deal to build a Trump Tower in Moscow.

RUSSIAN RUCTIONS IN TRUMP'S ELECTION CAMPAIGN

When Trump made his run for the presidency, a volley of pro-Moscow remarks and a slate of advisers with notable Russian connections rang alarm bells in Washington.

Vladimir Putin
Trump strikes a pro-Moscow tone

Trump attracted attention for multiple comments praising Vladimir Putin and his policies. Last December, Putin called Trump "talented", a compliment Trump described as a "great honour". This summer Trump appeared to incite Moscow to hack into Hillary Clinton's private emails. At a 2014 press lunch, Trump claimed to have spoken "indirectly and directly" with Putin, "who could not have been nicer". He subsequently denied ever meeting Putin.

Paul Manafort
Ex-chairman of Trump's campaign

Trump's campaign chairman Paul Manafort quit in August 2016 amid controversy over his work advising the pro-Moscow former president of Ukraine, Viktor Yanukovych. Ousted from power in 2014 amid allegations of massive embezzlement, Yanukovych fled to Russia. Ukrainian authorities found a ledger showing $12.7m in off-book payments to Manafort by Yanukovych's party, payments Manafort has strongly denied receiving. Manafort's interpreter had a background in Russian military intelligence, according to colleagues.

Carter Page
Trump's former foreign policy adviser

Manafort is not the only Trump adviser to quit over Russian links. Carter Page, a former Merrill Lynch banker and adviser to Russian state energy company Gazprom, was named by Trump as a foreign policy adviser. The New York Times has reported that FBI agents examined during the summer numerous possible connections between Russians and members of Mr. Trump's inner circle, including Mr Manafort and Mr Page, as well as a mysterious and unexplained trail of computer activity between the Trump Organization and an email account at a large Russian bank, Alfa Bank. Page resigned from the Trump campaign in September.

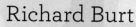

Richard Burt
The former ambassador with a Russian link

Richard Burt, an ex-US ambassador to Germany, helped draft a Trump foreign policy speech in April, while earning hundreds of thousands of dollars lobbying for a Russian-backed gas pipeline that would extend Putin's leverage over Europe. Burt told the FT he was "not in any way officially involved" with Trump's campaign, but provided "some ideas or language" for the speech. Burt advises the owners of Russia's Alfa Group, who have close Kremlin ties.

Michael Flynn
The ex-general paid to attend a Moscow banquet

Michael Flynn, a former head of the US Defense Intelligence Agency, was named as a national security adviser by the Trump campaign and was nominated by Mr Trump in November to take that role in government. Like Trump, Flynn has argued for closer links with Russia. In interviews, Flynn acknowledged being paid to give a speech and attend a lavish anniversary party for the state-controlled RT television network in Moscow, where he sat next to President Putin.

THE OUTSIDE VIEW

Michael D'Antonio
Author of "The Truth About Trump"

Michael D'Antonio, author of "The Truth About Trump", believes the Republican contender is drawn to Russian oligarchs' aggression and toughness as well as their wealth. "He's practically Donald the Red," he said. "He is very much focused on Russia and it certainly causes a person to wonder why."

David Cay Johnston
Author of "The Making of Donald Trump"

David Cay Johnston, who wrote "The Making of Donald Trump", a biography, believes the full story about Trump and Russia has yet to be told. "Every time Vladimir Putin is mentioned, Trump goes out of his way to express deep respect for him, which suggests there's something very important which we simply don't know," he said.

Michael McFaul
Former US ambassador to Russia

Michael McFaul, who advised the Obama White House on Russia before taking up his diplomatic post, says Trump's policy statements on Russia are "frightening". "Does Putin prefer that Trump would win the election? Absolutely yes," he told the FT. "Why wouldn't he want Trump to be president? He's said things that support his policy." McFaul concluded: "There's a lot we don't know."

WHAT DO TRUMP AND HIS ORGANISATION SAY?

Michael Cohen
Executive vice-president and special counsel, the Trump Organization

"The Trump Organization does not have any properties in Russia and the press' [sic] fascination with this narrative is both misleading and fabricated. Perpetuation of this false connection...or any connection with Russia altogether – is yet another example of the press's liberal bias towards Mr Trump."

Donald Trump
In the 2nd presidential debate, discussing hacking of Democratic Party systems

"Maybe there is no hacking but they always blame Russia and the reason is because they think they're trying to tarnish me with Russia. I know about Russia, but I know nothing about the inner workings of Russia. I have no businesses, I have no loans from Russia."

On December 12, Mr Trump said the CIA's reported claims of Russian hacking to favour his election were "ridiculous", telling Fox News: "I think it's just another excuse. I don't believe it." He also revealed that he had rejected daily intelligence briefings, in part because he was a "smart person".

MUELLER REPORT, VOLUME 2

Justice does not exist for the President to control or dictate its terms. Congress is a coequal branch of government with subpoena powers. If any person resists a subpoena, they are in contempt of Congress and can be jailed. There are procedures to be followed. We are a Country that is defined by our Laws.

Volume 2 of the Mueller Report sets up the Impeachment case against Donald Trump, citing many instances of Obstruction of Justice. In addition, recent alleged actions by the President of Obstruction of Justice may be added to Robert Mueller's list of offenses. "We the People" have been harmed and our very survival depends on the President, his Cabinet and co-conspirators being removed from office before they cause further weakening of our Democracy and ourselves.

Notes on the Mueller Report, Volume 2:

1. The Trump Campaign's response to Russian interference in our Elections was confirmed by individuals within the Trump organization and the FBI.

2. Trump lied about his ongoing pursuit of the Moscow Tower with the potential to net him billions with little risk. Americans *must question his legitimacy* after a foreign power, Russia, contributed monetary assistance to his campaign.

3. The fact that Trump denied these facts and publicly waged a campaign against The Special Counsel <u>constitutes, in my opinion, Obstruction of Justice.</u>

4. Trump's tweets should be included in evidence as his many attempts to disparage this investigation and their findings.

5. Russia did interfere in US Elections, violating the privacy of individuals connected to voter registration rolls and others not connected to the Trump Campaign.

6. Individuals connected to the Trump Campaign separately told the President in March and April (2016) that Wikileaks had the emails for which Trump was searching. This was no witch hunt, nor is Russian interference in our Elections trivial.

7. On 6/14/16, The DNC independently conducted an in-house assessment of the DNC computers and found that they were hacked by the Russian Government.

8. On 7/22/16, Wikileaks dumped thousands of hacked DNC documents, timing their release for the beginning of the Democratic National Convention. The Trump Campaign and Trump were gleeful and encouraged Wikileaks to release more emails. Their exact words are redacted on p 17 under Section 11 of the Factual Results of the Obstruction Investigation.

9. Trump and members of his campaign knew Wikileaks had the emails of John Podesta and Hillary Clinton and were waiting for the proper timing of their release.

10. When Trump was asked about America's stance on Crimea, <u>he said he would recognize it as Russian territory.</u> He did not say that in his private communications with a Russian (Kirill Dmitriev). He was anticipating building a Real Estate complex there, like those in the Ukraine & Georgia. The prize was Moscow Tower and a Letter of Intent was signed with the Russians by Donald Trump Jr & Ivanka Trump, acting on Trump's behalf. <u>His policy toward the Ukraine was changed and softened language was entered into the RNC platform.</u>

11. Trump sent Michael Flynn to delay UN votes.

12. Trump deflected his involvement with Russia by asking Wikileaks to leak "dirt" on the Clinton Foundation. He constantly denied his involvement with Russia and Russians close to Putin.

13. The only spin job came from Trump and his campaign as they actively pursued ties to Russia for their own monetary gain.

    • Russia is a Kleptocracy; aren't we becoming a Plutocracy?

14. The President directed his counsel, Donald McGahn, to stop AG Sessions from legally recusing himself from the Russian Investigation.

15. Mueller investigated the President 's conduct concerning the Investigation of Michael Flynn who had personal contact, as directed by the Trump Transition Team, with Sergey Kislyak, Russia's Ambassador to the US.

16. Flynn called Kislyak and requested that Russia not escalate the situation concerning Sanctions. Responding to Trump's anger, Flynn said the conversation never happened.

17. On 1/26/17, Sally Yates contacted McGahn to inform him there was an FBI Investigation on Flynn and confirmed the conversation with Kislyak that Flynn was denying.

    • McGahn tells the President, who asks about the Law. Did Flynn violate the Espionage Act?

18. On 1/27/17, the President invites James Comey to the White House and asks him to stop investigating Flynn.

19. By 2/2/17, it is confirmed that Flynn had lied about his talks with Kislyak.

20. When Flynn recounted truthfully to the President the dates that he'd discussed with Kislyak, the President corrected one of his dates.

    - How did Trump know the exact dates and conversations taking place, unless he had listening devices on all his employees?

    - On 3/13, Flynn was fired. When the President hears Flynn is going to testify before the FBI and Congressional Investigators, the President said Flynn should testify and that everyone, even Democrats are after him. The President continues to speak to Flynn, telling him to stay strong. By encouraging Flynn in this way, isn't Trump obstructing justice?

21. Jeff Sessions, when becoming AG, was forced to recuse himself, because he had had numerous contacts with Kislyak.

22. The President was furious with AG Sessions because he recused himself and displayed his anger and displeasure on numerous public and private occasions, demeaning and disparaging AG Sessions for acting in accordance with the law. The President's behavior is improper, unethical and justifies Obstruction of Justice charges.

23. When the President reached out to Dan Coats, Mike Pompeo, Mike Rogers and Comey, following Comey's public announcement of the FBI's Russia Investigation, it is relevant and helps us to understand the motivation of other actions towards the Investigation.

24. The President was focused on the Russia Investigation and its implications for his Presidency. The President was concerned that if the Public believed Russia helped him with the election, it would detract from his accomplishments.

25. On 5/3/17, Comey testified before Congress and declined to discuss the scope of the Russia Investigation. The President was angered by Comey's "non-compliance" with his wishes and fired him on 5/9/17 without the consent of the DOJ at the time.

26. Then the President tried to defame Comey's character. Before defaming Comey and firing him, he tried to deflect criticism of his firing by saying it was Rod Rosenstein and Session's

idea. Yet, he knew, and his staff knew, the President, wished to remove Comey, thinking falsely that the Russia Investigation would go away. (In my opinion, the Investigation continues to show President Trump to be a person who lies & dissembles the truth!)

27. Speaking on TV to journalist Lester Holt, Trump stated that the Russian Investigation is a made-up story, an excuse by the Democrats for having lost the election that they should have won.

28. By firing Comey, Trump was aware he might lengthen the Investigation. That is Obstruction of Justice, with knowledge that you're causing Obstruction. In fact, the next day, the President tweeted, the Russians must be laughing, as the US tears itself apart over a "democratic excuse" for losing the election. He keeps up his tweets, knowing all along that Comey headed the FBI's Russian Investigation, and Comey's removal would impede and obstruct the Investigation.

29. As Mueller gains a greater understanding of Trump's paranoia re Russia's interference in our Election, we know that witnesses stated Trump was aware that Russian Intelligence officers were behind hacks and he was awaiting future Wikileaks releases. The President was preoccupied with press coverage of the Russian Investigation and the Public's perception of his legitimacy.

30. On 5/17/17, Rod Rosenstein appointed a Special Counsel to oversee the Investigation. On 6/14/17, the press reported that the President is being investigated for Obstruction of Justice.

31. Because of Comey's firing, the FBI delivered a preservation notice to McGahn, instructing the White House to preserve all relevant documents concerning Comey's firing. McGahn issued a document hold and instructed staff that nothing was to be burned, pending his review.

32. On 5/18/17, Sessions tendered his resignation for the first time! The President shook Sessions hand and kept the letter. On 5/30/17, the President returned Sessions' letter of resignation.

33. Next, Trump ruminated on the firing of the Special Counsel. Then he went on the attack. Tweeting, "They made up a phony collusion story with the Russians, found zero. So now they go for Obstruction of Justice on the phony story. Nice." Then he states, "...Witch Hunt led by bad and conflicted people."

34. When we review the President's direction to McGahn to fire the Special Counsel, there is clear evidence for Obstruction of Justice.

35. Trump directed McGahn to call Dep AG Rosenstein to fire the Special Counsel. The President urged McGahn to do this immediately on a Saturday. Remove Mueller. The only reason the President would have had for removing Mueller was because he feared a foreseeable Grand Jury proceeding.

36. All of Trump's acts, his calls, his tweets, and his attempt to fire Mueller weighed on his mind. Then, he learns Flynn is in the Special Counsel's "cross hairs". Mueller went after Flynn for good reason. Flynn was the point man for Russia, asking them not to retaliate for Obama's sanctions. Flynn indicated that Trump would take care of them (sanctions) with Putin when he's President.

37. By June 17, 2017 Trump is now faced with an investigation he didn't want, but by his own actions forced. The Special Counsel was now investigating him "for the crazy shit" he asked of everyone.

38. Next, on 6/19/17, he dictates a letter to Corey Lewandowski, saying he had no connection with the Russians. Yet, his children were busy saying they got encrypted messages from Wikileaks, acknowledging their receipt and release of sensitive emails by Podesta and Clinton, with instructions on retweets and Trump is cheering them on!

39. Also, on 6/19/17, the June 9th, 2016 Trump Tower meeting is aired in the press, stating that several Russians met with Jared Kushner, Trump Jr and Ron Goldstone etc. to get dirt on Clinton. On that same date, Lewandowski is summoned to the White House and again, he is on the hook. He never gave the President's note to AG Sessions, nor did he fire Sessions or ask him to stop the Investigation.

40. Next, the President gives an impromptu interview to The NY Times telling the Public he's angry with Sessions for having recused himself from the Russian Investigation. Based on Sessions' associations with the Russians, he had to recuse himself. He had no choice.

41. Three days later, it was discovered by the Washington Post, that US intelligence intercepts showed that Sessions had discussed polling data with the Russian Ambassador, contrary to what he had stated publicly. P 96

42. Trump, sends a message through Lewandowski to Sessions to stop his recusal and confine his Investigation. Mueller discusses this matter as an Obstruction of Justice charge. The President had wanted through Sessions' actions, to eliminate Mueller, and secure all future

elections. The Grand Jury was convened, and the President wanted to limit its scope. The President sought to remove any investigation of himself and the campaign team.

43. Trump ordered AG Sessions to restrict and redirect 2 days after McGahn had refused to give the same order.

44. Evidently, Clinton's emails were also the subject of the June 9th meeting. Trump then dictated a letter to Trump Jr. stating that the meeting was about adoption, which was an outright lie! The Chief Prosecutor of Russia was supplying emails of Clinton and her dealings with Russia. Trump denied all knowledge of these emails.

45. By this time, all documents relating to Trump, the Campaign and any Russians were to be turned over to the Special Prosecutor's office.

46. Disingenuously, Reince Priebus and the attorneys heard about the information from Fox News. The President directs his Communications staff to not publicly disclose information on the June 9th meeting. Jared and Ivanka Kushner had the emails and wanted to show them to Trump. He stated he was uninterested. But he already knew about them. He was concerned that the emails would leak.

47. Hope Hicks & Kushner wanted to release the emails and Trump said no. The President told Hicks to confine her statements to adoption. Trump Jr amended the letter to say it was primarily about adoption and covered up the real information of getting "dirt" on Clinton. (A NY Times article about the June 9th meeting may be accessed on the Internet, via the link below. The article dated 7/8/17, is entitled, "Trump team met with Lawyer linked to Kremlin during the Campaign) https://www.nytimes.com/2017/07/08/us/politics/trump-russia-kushner-manafort.html

48. That may be where "Dirty Hillary" originated. Their letter to the Times never mentioned the Magnitsky Act, Sanctions or Clinton. Hicks was concerned Priebus knew and there could be a leak.

49. The attorney, Mark Corallo, gave the real story about the June 9th meeting to the Times, introducing the Steele Dossier, to discredit Hillary Clinton and deflect the Russian connection from Trump. Actually, the GOP commissioned the Steele Dossier for use as opposition research during the Republican Primary. After Trump became the nominee, the Clinton campaign continued to fund op research through the Dossier.

50. The ongoing Grand Jury Investigation was redacted, presumably because it involves Trump Jr et al. Trump later denied knowledge of the 6/9/16 meeting.

51. On 7/9, David Wright says the President was unaware of the 6/9 meeting. The documents leaked. The attempt at Obstruction didn't occur. Though the emails about Clinton were damaging, it shows bad character, but not Obstruction.

52. After years of harassing Sessions, on 11/7/18, the President removes Sessions (Sessions resigns).

      • Next, Trump wants McGahn to state that he never tried to fire Mueller. Obstruction?

53. Trump's conduct toward Flynn, Manafort and one other is redacted, as "harm to an ongoing matter". Is it Rick Gates?

54. In January 2018, Manafort told Gates not to plead because he had been told by Trump that he would be taken care of! Trump knew Manafort for years. In 1988, Trump got him a VIP pass to the RNC.

55. Trump still talked about a rigged witch hunt to help Manafort's case. Mueller was angry and said Manafort had breached his plea agreement; he had lied to protect the President. The President and the Russians said he'd be taken care of. Manafort had no reason to cooperate. Trump is proud that Manafort, Jerome Corsi and one other never gave Mueller anything. Since these men may be operating under promises of pardons, this could also be a case for Obstruction of Justice by the President.

56. Trump stated a pardon is not off the table for Manafort. (Though, if he's impeached, all promised pardons are null and void) Redactions for Harm to an ongoing matter p 128. Corsi is connected to WikiLeaks p129. P130 is totally redacted.

57. Protection of Trump by AG Barr may result in Obstruction charges as well. The President's statement during the ongoing Jury trials could also have influenced the outcomes. In my opinion, the President's warning statements about Flynn could have kept Flynn lying and, therefore, obstructing Justice. One half of p134 is redacted, Harm to ongoing matter. This may be Mueller 's explanation of evidence and determination.

58. In April 2018, when Cohen's house was searched by the FBI, the President said Cohen would not flip. This is the same tactic he used with Flynn and Flynn did not flip.

59. By July 2018, Cohen had cooperated, and Trump called him a rat.

60. The Trump Moscow deal looms large, at least $2 Billion, with little risk for Trump.

- One must ask how dependent on Putin is Trump? He authorized the signing of the LOI by Trump, Jr and Ivanka, with the help of Felix Sater, a Russian intermediary with The Crocus Group.

61. Cohen reaches out directly to the office of Dimitry Peskov and his call is returned. Shortly afterwards, Slater calls saying Vladimir Putin had called. On 5/16, Cohen asks Trump about a trip to Moscow to move the project forward. It was agreed that Cohen would go to Moscow before the Convention and Trump would go afterward. They're invited to the St. Petersburg Forum on June 16, 2016.

62. Trump was now distancing himself from Russia. Curiously, as part of an agreed script to distance Trump from Russia, Trump minimized the Trump Tower Project, in accordance with the "Party Line" he had developed. Trump and Cohen were now joined in defense, which was bad for Cohen. Cohen was told to reach out to Putin when he was at the UN on 9/15. This predates the Letter of Intent signing in 2016.

63. Distancing Trump from Russia was not possible, since Cohen was in daily contact with Trump's Counsel. After Cohen admitted to lying, Mueller reached out to Trump's personal Counsel, who would not communicate with him, citing privilege! In these matters, there is no privilege, if the House starts the Impeachment proceedings based on the Obstruction case. Going before Congress negates privilege.

64. Cohen constantly reflected on how he would stay on message to protect Trump and the Tower. His legal expenses were covered by the Trump Organization. (This was legal since he was a senior member of that organization.)

65. Cohen was following Kushner's lead. Make statements in advance and lie. Lay the groundwork for a cover up. After lying to Congress, Cohen spoke to the President's Counsel.

66. Campaign Finance violations were found when the Stormy Daniels check is found.

67. There are more lies, before the truth comes out. Trump calls Cohen a good man. In Trump's world, the good men are Flynn, Manafort, and Cohen. They stick together in their lying. An anonymous personal Trump friend (who?) calls Cohen to reassure him that the boss loves him – this is redacted, presumably to shield Trump.

68. Again, Trump stated that Cohen will not flip. Cohen felt it was in his best interest to tow the party line. He needed Trump. When Trump was asked about pardons for Manafort & Cohen, he said it was too early to talk about them. That was on 6/8/18.

69. By 7/2/18, Cohen was cooperating with the Special Counsel. One piece of evidence from the FBI raid on Cohen's offices, etc., was a recording between Trump and Cohen re payoffs to a second woman. This represented additional campaign finance violations!

70. The notes on the June 9th meeting surfaced, including talks with Trump Jr and dirt on Clinton. The Investigation turned to the Trump Tower Moscow Project and still on script, Cohen lied, stating it had been abandoned on 12/3/18. Trump's rant is redacted as "harm to an ongoing matter".

71. Rudy Giuliani talks about Trump Tower Moscow. He cleared the record and stated talks were ongoing up to the Election. Then Giuliani retracts and says his remarks were hypothetical. P152

   • Mueller questions whether there is evidence to show that Cohen and Trump got their stories straight with Trump's participation.

72. Cohen spoke to the President's Counsel about Congressional testimony. The Party line was discussed with Trump's Counsel, who is immune, if a criminal case is brought, but not if proceedings leading to Impeachment, are started by The House.

73. In my opinion, they should subpoena all relevant parties after starting the procedures leading toward Impeachment. The Trump Tower property is not trivial. P 154.

74. There is evidence that Trump knew that Cohen made false statements about the Moscow project and he did so to protect the President and minimize the connection between Trump and Russia.

   • When Cohen flipped, The President knowingly tried to harm Cohen and his family, showing him what happens when you thwart him. Isn't that witness tampering or obstructing justice? Aren't they scare tactics to prevent the witness from cooperating? P156

75. The definition of Obstruction of Justice: If someone is motivated by a desire to protect non-criminal personal interests, to protect against Investigations where the underlying criminal liability falls into a grey area, or to avoid personal embarrassment, may have committed obstruction of justice. The injury to the integrity of the justice system is the same regardless of whether a person committed an underlying wrong.

76. The Investigation concluded that Trump's personal conduct called into question the legitimacy of Mueller's Investigation and continues to do so because Trump fears that the legitimacy of his Election is questioned & fears the uncertainty about the impact of certain events, where he had knowledge of their existence.

77. Many of the President's acts before the Public to prevent witnesses from "flipping" or cooperating with the Special Counsel can be construed as Obstruction. Considering the President has access to Public Communications and can amplify his wishes and concerns makes his behavior, if not criminal, obstructing. If the likely effect of the acts is to intimidate witnesses or alter testimony, the integrity of the justice system is equally threatened.

78. You have Flynn, Manafort, Cohen and others being influenced by the President, as he tries to obstruct justice and impede the Grand Jury proceedings.

    • It is important to view the President's behavior, not just the behavior of Flynn and Comey. What has Trump done?

79. The President has turned a blind eye toward Russian interference in our Election because he potentially will benefit from his relationship with them. When and if Trump Tower Moscow becomes a reality, he personally stands to make Billions, with zero risk.

80. McGahn was directed to remove the Special Counsel.

81. Then, Lewandowski was asked by the President to have AG Sessions remove his recusal and limit the scope of the Investigation.

82. Both acts were related and were indeed an attempt to prevent the Investigation from continuing.

83. Based on the evidence, the people charged with following the President's orders were not charged. However, the finger of attempted Obstruction of Justice resides with the President. P158

84. The last paragraph of this page lays out the Obstruction case. There were targeted efforts to remove the Special Counsel; POTUS requested the AG to revise and limit the scope of the Investigation; his team tried to prevent the 6/9/16 Trump Tower meeting information from coming out. The President used public forums to attack or praise witnesses in order to skew their testimony favorable to him. He intended to reward them, if they lied on his behalf. If

they didn't, they were threatened. The President knowingly obstructed justice and potentially influenced members of the Grand Jury by using the Bully Pulpit.

85. Mueller tells us which Statutes to use, when proceeding with the Obstruction Case. The Law, 18 U.S.C., 1512 (c) provides: **Whoever corruptly alters, destroys, mutilates or conceals a record, document or other document or attempts to do so, with the intent to impair the object's integrity or availability for use in a proceeding or otherwise obstructs, influences or impedes any official proceeding or attempts to do so, shall be fined under this title or imprisoned, not more than 20 yrs. or both. This Law applies to all corrupt means of obstructing a proceeding, pending or contemplated.**

86. Including using official power, Congress has specifically prohibited witness tampering. Trump has done that several times. Action 1512(c)1 specifically includes the requirement that the defendant act with the intent to impair the object's integrity or availability for use in an official proceeding.

87. A requirement that Congress also included in 2 other sections of 1512(b)2(B) use of intimidation, threats, corrupt persuasion, or misleading conduct with intent to cause a person to destroy an object, with the intent to impair the integrity or availability of the object for use in an official proceeding.

88. To appear before Congress in an Obstruction of Justice case the person does not need to have corrupt intent; he or she merely must intend to impair a proceeding.

89. Congress acted deliberately when they looked at conduct Section 1512(c)(2), addressing conduct specifically: obstructing, influencing or impeding a proceeding.

90. The purpose of mentioning these sections of the Law, is clarification. In sections, 1512(c)(1) vs 1513(c)(2), they are coequal when determining conduct. Destruction of physical evidence with intent to impair, as well as conduct that intends to impair a proceeding. If you do both, that's worse. <u>But one or the other is appropriate for Congress to proceed with the Obstruction of Justice Case.</u>

91. 1512(c)(2) Therefore, the Courts have broadly defined Obstruction and look at Obstruction in any form.

92. The President's conduct personally took many forms. From personal insults to praise, to using Social Media, to using surrogates to carry out his dirty work, to going to the newspapers

(though he calls them "enemies of the people"), he has no problem using them, when he wants to subvert justice. Trump uses the printed press or TV to get his message out.

93. Section 1512(c)(2) can be used against AG Barr and Treasury Secretary Steven Mnuchin, as well for conduct that impedes, obstructs or influences any official proceeding. 1513(c)(2) has been used in the courts and upheld convictions for conduct that thwarted investigations or arrests. Whereas (c)(1) is used for conduct that impairs the availability or integrity of documents or records.

94. The other basis for impeachment under Obstruction of Justice or high crimes and misdemeanors relates to tipping off the people being investigated and thereby hampering the Grand Jury process.

95. Therefore, 1512(c)(2) refers to corrupt acts including public officials that threaten the commencement or conduct of a proceeding and not just the acts that make evidence unavailable or impair the integrity of a proceeding.

96. These are grave and serious discoveries on my part. I am not an attorney, yet, I understand that the President can be brought before Congress on serious charges of Obstruction of Justice and High Crimes & misdemeanors. When, by his conduct, he intended to hinder the ongoing investigation of the Special Counsel and additionally, by his continued Public Campaign, may have thwarted the cases brought before the Grand Jury by interfering directly in witness testimony. Very serious! P156-163.

97. Mueller continues to lay out his legal case on p163, directing us to 18 U.S.C. Section 1503. It generally prohibits conduct that interferes with the administration of Justice.

98. Section 1512(c)(2) in Federal Obstruction of Justice Statutes captures corrupt conduct, other than document Obstruction, that has the natural tendency to obstruct, contemplated, as well as, pending proceedings. This Law overlaps with Section 1503 which is pending grand jury and judicial proceedings & 1505 pending administrative & Congressional proceedings.

99. In Section 1519, the Law states (The witness must merely have the intent to obstruct Justice, even if unsuccessful.) Congress doesn't need to prove a link between intent and conduct, as long as the conduct was seen to be directed at skewing the official proceedings. When charging, Mueller recommends noting the overlap between Sections 1503,1505 & 1519, meaning that section 1512(c)(2) may be broadly interpreted. He continues by stating that Congress enacted Section 1512(c)(2) as part of the Sarbanes Oxley act of 2002, under George

W Bush. Tampering with a record or otherwise impeding an official proceeding. Section 1512(c) was added by the Senate to close loopholes, such as document shredding. Both houses of Congress memorialized the unambiguous statutory text.

100. Therefore, both houses of Congress memorialized 1512(c)(2) prohibiting corruptly, obstructing, influencing, or impeding any official proceeding or attempting to do so. The Senate Committee explained that: the purpose of preventing an Obstruction or miscarriage of justice, cannot be fully carried out by a simple enumeration of the commonly prosecuted Obstruction offenses.

101. There must also be protection against the "rare type of conduct that is the product of the inventive criminal mind" and which also thwarts justice. This was verbatim. It's disingenuous for any branch of Government to call this investigation a witch hunt or partisan, since the Law was written and ratified by both houses of Congress in 2002 with a REPUBLICAN MAJORITY!

102. The Supreme Court has deferred to Congress in defining crimes and giving fair warning of what a criminal statute prohibits. However, Congress' interpretation supersedes all others, because it assumes the person had the intent to obstruct justice in mind.

103. Justice Scalia agreed with Congress and the interpretation "it denotes an act by an official that is inappropriate or inconsistent with official duty, giving them the advantage and influences the rights of others. Paraphrase p166.

104. Other Obstruction might apply to the conduct in this investigation. However, Mueller laid out his Case for Congress to act based on the Merit of the case Law.

105. The President has the obligation to take care that the Laws be faithfully executed. His behavior makes a mockery of our Laws and the Constitution. Those powers and duties form the basis of prosecutorial discretion.

106. The President's powers coexist with Congress, when they do not coexist to protect "We the people" from a President who obstructs justice and has the intent to harm Grand Jury proceedings and other investigations, then the two branches of Government must separate.

107. The Law is clear. If the President, in his official capacity, attempted to impede, interfere, or influence the outcome of an official proceeding, or inquiry, any committee or subcommittee is empowered, in either house or jointly, to bring an action of Obstruction of Justice. Therefore, Congress can regulate the President's actions, without harming his official capacity.

108. Congress may criminalize certain obstructive conduct of a President, if he is found to be suborning perjury, intimidating witnesses or fabricating evidence. All these occurred, time and again.

109. **<u>Separation of Powers Principles</u>** Supports the conclusion that Congress may validly prohibit Corrupt Obstructive Acts to be carried out through the President's official powers. p171 or 383 of the entire Mueller Report concluded that Congress may make a case for Obstruction of Justice without harming the President's Article 2 functions. That's the case. (P171 or p 383). Depending on whether you're reading volume 2 or the entire "pdf").

110. The Supreme Court's separation Of Powers balancing test applies in this Context. The Supreme Court has upheld that they are entitled to archival Presidential records, despite a claim by the President of Privilege.

111. Additionally, even when we take the many powers of the President into account, Congress' powers, in its separate role as Lawmaker, gives it substantial authority to determine, if the President's policy was just & proper. Congress may regulate the President's ability to act on his policies, if not on his ability to function. (P 173 /p385).

112. Nothing in the Constitution states that the President may use the power of a pardon to act corruptly or falsely. Congress has the power to prohibit the corrupt use of anything of value to influence the testimony of another person in a judicial, congressional or investigative proceeding.

113. Noting the Law, 18U.S.C. Section 201(b)(3) which includes the offer or promise of a pardon for providing false testimony or no testimony at all. The offer of a pardon would proceed the act and thus be within Congress' power to regulate, even if the Act of Pardoning is not. Therefore, this too, falls under the purview of the Obstruction of Justice statutes and does not interfere with the separation of powers. According to, and in support of, The Supreme Court has found no instance where charging a President with Obstruction of Justice interferes with a President's powers. The President has no more rights than an ordinary citizen to impede official proceedings by corruptly influencing witness testimony. (Page 173 or p386) The conduct is improper.

114. Congress as a body has failed to regulate the removal or the qualifications of members of the Executive Branch. There are no job descriptions for the President and his Cabinet. Cabinet members may be crooks and thieves, have conflicts of interest and even destroy the Institutions they were sworn to uphold. There has never been a limit imposed on chicanery.

115. Very interesting, though Congress may not remove or add Senior officers or Cabinet members, they may appoint junior officers to oversee Cabinet members as stated in the Constitution.

116. Inferior officers are the head of the FBI and the Special Counsel, each of whom reports to the AG. The Congress has the power to protect Congressional, Grand Jury and Judicial Proceedings against corrupt acts from any source. Therefore, Congress is entitled to a totally unredacted copy of Mueller's Report.

117. There is no argument. This is a proper request to safeguard the Law and within Congress' purview. The Obstruction of Justice statute necessitates that all material be made available to protect among other things, the integrity of its own proceedings, Grand Jury Investigations and Federal Criminal trials.

118. No one wants to go to the lengths of charging the President with Obstruction of Justice. However, unless or until they do, they are not entitled to a full unredacted copy of the Mueller Report. We don't need to "spin our wheels" to prevent name calling of the House, as partisan Democrats. To preserve the Rule of Law and the Integrity of our Democracy, "We the People" must take a stand for Justice. In our own defense and for our own salvation, we must call for Impeachment on the grounds of Obstruction of Justice.

119. Going back to 1831, there is a long precedent for maintaining the rights of Congress to act appropriately to save its own legislative functions. It may act against a President who would impede fact gathering and lawmaking efforts. Congress also has the power to protect the judiciary from obstructive acts by the Attorney General.

120. In the Supreme Court case against Nixon, the need to safeguard judicial integrity is a compelling Constitutional imperative. Note: the denial of full disclosure of the facts surrounding relevant communications of the President threatens the integrity of the judicial system and public confidence in the system.

121. Ultimately, justice will be done. Richard Nixon's AG John Mitchell was found guilty of Obstruction of Justice. He blocked the release of the Pentagon Papers and was found guilty and sent to prison.

122. Mueller writes that we are entitled to see the Grand Jury Investigation to determine if others should be indicted. That's vital to the criminal justice process.

123. It is imperative that "We the People" support the actions of the House Judiciary Committee. To do less, after knowing the facts would be a crime. (P177 or p 389)

124. After reading Mueller's legal brief, I am convinced that everyone in this land must call upon Congress to commence Impeachment proceedings. No less than our Democracy depends on this.

125. p183 or p 395 begins Appendix A & Mueller concludes his Investigation after approximately 2 years, which began on 5/17/17.

126. Appendix B is a Glossary of referenced persons, organizations and acronyms. All worthwhile "refreshers of information" and an understanding of the scope of the Mueller Report. The Russian connections outweigh the American principals involved.

127. Appendix C restates Mueller's strategy. It appears from the redaction on p 418, Trump is the subject of the Grand Jury Investigation. Mueller considered issuing a subpoena for his testimony but wrapped up the case instead. He knew that he had enough information from other sources to allow him to draw relevant factual conclusions on intent and credibility, which are often inferred from circumstantial evidence & assessed without direct testimony.

128. As part of the Appendix C, there are written questions asked of Trump, to which he must respond under oath. Besides the legal roadmap setting up the validity of an Impeachment proceeding for Obstruction of Justice, Appendix C's questions for the President are a legal route to discovery. These questions are mostly answered under both volumes 1 & 2, referring to Russian Collusion and the case for Obstruction.

129. We know from corroborated testimony that Donald Trump's answers to Mueller's questions on the June 9th meeting were lies.

130. Appendix D P444 states "Harm to Ongoing Matter", titled: Investigation ongoing; re: Manafort & his connections with Ukrainian ex- President. Information on Roger Stone is redacted. Referrals to the FBI can be gathered independent of the AG, by Congress, because the FBI are considered inferior members of the Administration.

131. Of the 14 people referred to the FBI or other appropriate Law enforcement entities, criminal activity was identified but outside the scope of the Special Counsel. 13 persons are redacted by Barr, the current AG.

132. My conclusions:

   ✓ Congress should continue empowering the Grand Jury and seek all relevant testimony!

✓ Congress should Impeach Trump in order to obtain the total unredacted work product of the Special Counsel and ultimately seek justice for all Americans.

✓ The scope of Mueller's Investigation is enormous and encompasses approximately 140 individuals, of whom 70% are Russian.

Editorial by Joyce Silver

The Redacted Mueller Report

The redactions raise many *critical* questions:

- Since we are aware that The Russian Internet Agency (GRU) interfered in our 2016 election and they started work on their campaign in 2014, why are sections redacted that would enable the Public to understand their methodology in undermining our Democracy?

- Why aren't all their Facebook, Twitter and Social Media sites available for public scrutiny?

- Once available to us through Mueller's Report, have they been totally removed from the relevant Social Media platforms?

- Will someone be watching for future foreign interference in our Elections and will the foreign actors be sanctioned? Will the Candidate being helped, be disqualified?

- Why shouldn't we understand who was targeted, how many Americans were targeted, and if they're still being targeted? Were Russian Voting machines used? If so, in which States?

- Why don't we have full disclosure of their methodology?

- How did the Russians pay for these ads?

- Who saw them and how many times were actions taken in response?

The American People are entitled to the truth. It's disheartening that all pages dealing with specific instances of Russian interference and using our social media, is redacted in its entirety!

- Why? They claim **"harm to an ongoing matter"**. What does that mean? If the Russian sites still exist, wouldn't you expect them to be gearing up to help Trump in 2020?

- Why should a free Democracy allow this interference to occur again?

What did Mueller find:

✓ Day to day recruitment for political rallies.

✓ Recruitment of people to amplify the Russian message.

✓ The Russians paid for plane tickets and bullhorns for rallies.

✓ They also paid for rally supplies.

✓ The Trump Campaign then retweeted the tweets from the Russian sites.

✓ Along with Brian Pascale who was hired to run Trump's social media campaign, Trump spent $70 million on Social Media and used the Russian media sites to make himself look good and smear Hillary Clinton.

✓ One site used by Donald Trump and his Campaign included Trump Jr. @Ten GOP.

Still more questions are raised. Our Democracy stands, *buffeted by a Republican Party that continues to hold this President above the Law.* The Constitution protects us by giving the Congress oversight of the executive branch through impeachment. Impeachment is the only remedy available to "We the People" to protect our Democracy and the Rule of Law.

It is the People's responsibility to demand Impeachment based on the Sections of Obstruction of Justice. Look on the bright side. More people may be swayed to change alliances, when confronted by the facts outlined in the Mueller Report.

- Don't be political. Act now to demand equal justice under the Law and the preservation of our Democracy.

Otherwise, it will more than likely be two more years of an empowered President and his administration, or potentially six more years and "We the People" may not survive. What could happen is that we continue to suffer from income inequality and climate catastrophes, exacerbated by Late Stage Capitalism's quest for short term gains. Our very survival is at stake. We can no longer complacently sit back and let "Nature" take its course. Why be nihilistic, when we have the capacity to innovate for change and our survival?

- How many more catastrophes do we need before we get over fatalism and say **Enough?**

- Will fracking near Yosemite or other locations in the country, turn you into an activist?

- Will overturning the ACA (Affordable Care Act) turn you into an Activist? Or will you allow millions of Americans to lose the health care coverage they now have?

- Will the "China Trade Wars" turn you into an Activist? The American Consumer, not China will pay for these tariffs, I promise!

- How much suffering do we have to endure before we say **Enough?**

- Do the American People and the rest of humanity have to "face" the horrific times above, before we overwhelmingly support the House of Representatives' starting the Investigation leading to Impeachment of this President, who acts as if he's above the Law and disseminates the worst policy decisions since Herbert Hoover and Grover Cleveland?

Once the House opens an Obstruction of Justice Case, pending Impeachment, Congress becomes a coequal branch of Government, equal to the Executive Branch. At that point in time, once the Investigations proceed, an entire "Clean Copy" of Mueller's report becomes available to "We the People", along with all documents requested from Justice, Treasury, et al, plus attorney client privilege ceases to exist.

We already have a case for Obstruction of Justice, laid out by Mueller, with case law included and a roadmap to follow. Don't be like General McClellan (Who led the Union Armies during the Civil War), too cautious to seize the opportunity to act boldly. Do it now. Preserve the Constitution and Congress' right to be a respected coequal branch of Government.

If we don't impeach this president, we will have no one to blame but ourselves. Do it now for our children, our grandchildren and their children. Let's leave this World better than we found it!

GLOSSARY

The following glossary contains names and brief descriptions of individuals and entities that may or may not be referenced in the two volumes of this report

Agalarov, Aras	Russian real-estate developer (owner of the Crocus Group); met Donald Trump in connection with the Miss Universe pageant and helped arrange the June 9, 2016 meeting at Trump Tower between Natalia Veselnitskaya and Trump Campaign officials.
Assange, Julian	Founder of WikiLeaks, which in 2016 posted on the internet documents stolen from entities and individuals affiliated with the Democratic Party.
Bannon, Steve	White House chief strategist and senior counselor to President Trump (Jan. 2017-Aug. 2017); chief executive of the Trump Campaign
Barr, William	Acting Attorney General of the United States
Berkowitz, Avi	Assistant to Jared Kushner.
Boente, Dana	Acting Attorney General (Jan. 2017 - Feb. 2017); Acting Deputy Attorney General (Feb . 2017 - Apr. 2017)
Bossert, Thomas (Tom)	Former homeland security advisor to the President who also served as a senior official on the Presidential Transition Team.
Browder, William (Bill)	Founder of Hermitage Capital Management who lobbied in favor of the Magnitsky Act, which imposed financial and travel sanctions on Russian officials.
Calamari, Matt	Chief operating officer for the Trump Organization.
Caputo, Michael	Trump Campaign advisor.
Chaika, Yuri	Prosecutor general of the Russian Federation who also maintained a relationship with Aras Agalarov.
Christie, Chris	Former Governor of New Jersey.
Clapper, James	Director of National Intelligence (Aug. 2010 - Jan. 2017).
Clovis, Samuel Jr.	Chief policy advisor and national co-chair of the Trump Campaign.
Coats, Dan	Director of National Intelligence.
Cobb, Ty	Special Counsel to the President (July 2017 - May 2018).
Cohen, Michael	Former vice president to the Trump Organization and special counsel to Donald Trump who spearheaded an effort to build a Trump-branded property in Moscow. He admitted to lying to Congress about the project.
Comey, James Jr.	Director of the Federal Bureau of Investigation (Sept. 4, 2013 - May 9, 2017).

Conway, Kellyanne	Counselor to President Trump and manager of the Trump Campaign.
Corallo, Mark	Spokesman for President Trump's personal legal team (Jun 2017-Jul 2017)
Corsi, Jerome	Author and political commentator who formerly worked for WorldNetDaily and InfoWars. **Harm to Ongoing Matter**
Credico, Randolph	Radio talk show host who interviewed Julian Assange in 2016. **Harm to Ongoing Matter**
Dearborn, Rick	Former White House deputy chief of staff for policy who previously served as chief of staff to Senator Jeff Sessions.
Dempsey, Michael	Office of Director of National Intelligence Official who recalled discussions with Dan Coats after Coats' meeting with President Trump on March 22, 2017.
Deripaska, Oleg	Russian businessman with ties to Vladimir Putin who hired Paul Manafort for consulting work between 2005 and 2009.
Dmitriev, Kirill	Head of the Russian Direct Investment Fund (RDIF); met with Erik Prince in the Seychelles in January 2017 and, separately, drafted a US-Russia reconciliation plan with Rick Gerson.
Erchova, Lana (aka Lana Alexander	Ex-wife of Dmitry Klokov who emailed Ivanka Trump to introduce Klokov to the Trump Campaign in the fall of 2015.
Flynn, Michael Jr.	Son of Michael T. Flynn, National Security Advisor (Jan 20, 2017-Feb 13, 2017).
Flynn, Michael T.	National Security Advisor (Jan 20, 2017-Feb 13, 2017), Director of the Defense Intelligence Agency (July 2012-Aug 7, 2014), and Trump Campaign advisor. He pleaded guilty to lying to the FBI about communications with Ambassador Sergey Kislyak in December 2016.
Gates, Richard (Rick) III	Deputy campaign manager for the Trump campaign, Trump Inaugural Committee deputy chairman, and longtime employee of Paul Manafort. He pleaded guilty to conspiring to defraud the United States and violate US laws, as well as making false statements to the FBI.
Goldstone, Robert	Publicist for Emin Agalarov who contacted Donald Trump Jr. to arrange the June 9, 2016 meeting at Trump Tower between Natalia Veselnitskaya and Trump campaign officials.
Gorkov, Sergey	Chairman of Vnesheconombank (VEB), a Russian state-owned bank, who met with Jared Kushner during the transition period.
Hicks, Hope	White House communications director Aug 2017-Mar 2018) and press secretary for the Trump campaign.
Holt, Lester	NBC News anchor who interviewed President Trump on May 11, 2017.

Ivanov, Sergei	Special representative of Vladimir Putin, former Russian deputy prime minister, and former FSB deputy director. In January 2016, Michael Cohen emailed the Kremlin requesting to speak to Ivanov.
HOM	**Harm to Ongoing Matter**
Kelly, John	White House chief of staff (July 2017-Jan 2019)
Khalilzad, Zalmay	US special representative to Afghanistan and former US ambassador. He met with Senator Jeff Sessions during foreign policy dinners put together through the Center for the National Interest.
Kilimnik, Konstantin	Russian-Ukrainian political consultant and long-time employee of Paul Manafort assessed by the FBI to have ties to Russian Intelligence.
Kislyak, Sergey	Former Russian ambassador to the United States and current Russian senator from Mordovia.
Klokov, Dmitry	Executive for PJSC federal Grid Company of Unified Energy System and former aide to Russia's minister of energy. He communicated with Michael Cohen about a possible meeting between Vladimir Putin and candidate Trump.
Kushner, Jared	President Trump's son-in-law and senior advisor to the President.
Lavrov, Sergey	Russian minister of foreign affairs and former permanent representative of Russia to the United Nations.
Lewandowski Klokov, Corey	Campaign manager for the Trump Campaign (Jan 2015-June 2016)
Magnitsky, Sergei	Russian tax specialist who alleged Russian government corruption and died in Russian police custody in 2009. His death prompted passage of the Magnitsky Act, which imposed financial and travel sanctions on Russian officials.
Malloch, Ted	Chief executive officer of Global Fiduciary Governance and the Roosevelt Group. He was a London-based associate of Jerome Corsi.
Manafort, Paul Jr.	Trump campaign member (Mar 2016-Aug 2016) and chairman and chief strategist (May2016-Aug 2016).
McCabe, Andrew	Acting director of the FBI (May 2017-Aug 2017); deputy director of the FBI (Feb 2016-Jan 2018)
McGahn, Donald	White House Counsel (Jan 2017-Oct 2018)
Mifsud, Joseph	Maltese national and former London-based professor who, immediately after returning from Moscow in April 2016, told George Papadopoulos that the Russians had "dirt" in the form of thousands of Clinton emails.
Miller, Matt	Trump Campaign staff member who was present at the meeting of the National Security and Defense Platform Subcommittee in July 2016.

Miller, Stephen	Senior advisor to the President.
Mnuchin, Steven	Secretary of the Treasury
Nader, George	Advisor to the United Arab Emirates' Crown Prince who arranged a meeting between Kirill Dmitriev and Erik Prince during the transition period.
Page, Carter	Foreign policy advisor to the Trump campaign who advocated pro-Russian views and made July and December 2016 visits to Moscow.
Papadopoulos, George	Foreign policy advisor to the Trump campaign who received information from Joseph Mifsud that Russians had "dirt" in the form of thousands of Clinton emails. He pleaded guilty to lying to the FBI about his contact with Mifsud.
Podesta, John Jr.	Clinton campaign chairman whose email account was hacked by the GRU. WikiLeaks released his stolen emails during the 2016 campaign.
Polonskaya, Olga	Russian national introduced to George Papadopoulos by Joseph Mifsud as an individual with connections to Vladimir Putin.
Pompeo, Michael	US Secretary of State; Director of the Central Intellignece Agency (Jan 2017-Apr 2018).
Porter, Robert	White House staff secretary (Jan 2017-Feb 2018)
Priebus, Reince	White House chief of staff (Jan 2017-Jul 2017); chair of the Republican National Committee (Jan 2011-Jan 2017).
Prince, Erik	Businessman and Trump campaign supporter who met with presidential transition team officials after the election and traveled to the Seychelles to meet with Kirill Dmitriev in January 2017.
Rogers, Michael	Director of the National Security Agency (Apr 2014-May 2018).
Rosenstein, Rod	Deputy Attorney General (Apr 2017-present); Acting Attorney General for the Russian election interference investigation (May 2017-Nov 2018).
Sanders, Sarah Huckabee	White House press secretary (Jul 2017-Jun 2019)
Sater, Felix	Real-estate advisor who worked with Michael Cohen to pursue a Trump Tower Moscow project.
Sessions, Jefferson III	Attorney General (Feb 2017-Nov 2018); US Senator (Jan 1997-Feb 2017); head of the Trump Campaign's foreign policy advisory team.
Simes, Dimitri	President and chief executive officer of the Center for the National Interest.
Stone, Roger	Advisor to the Trump campaign. **Harm to Ongoing Matter**.
Tillerson, Rex	US Secretary of State (Feb 2017-Mar 2018

Trump, Donald Jr	President Trump's son; trustee and executive vice president of the Trump Organization; helped arrange and attended the June 9, 2016 meeting at Trump Tower between Natalia Veselnitskaya and Trump campaign officials.
Trump, Eric	President Trump's son; trustee and executive vice president of the Trump Organization.
Trump, Ivanka	President Trump's daughter; advisor to the President and former executive vice president of the Trump Organization.
Van der zwann, Alexander	Former attorney at Skadden, Arps, Slate, Meagher & Flom, LLP; worked with Paul Manafort and Rick Gates.
Veselnitskaya, Natalia	Russian attorney who was the principal speaker at the June 9, 2016 meeting at Trump Tower with Trump Campaign officials.
Yanukovych, Viktor	Former president of Ukraine who had worked with Paul Manafort.
Yates, Sally	Acting Attorney General (Jan 20, 2017-Jan 30, 2017); Deputy Attorney General (Jan 10, 2015-Jan 30, 2017).
Entities and Organizations	
Crocus Group	A Russian real-estate and property development company that, in 2013 hosted the Miss Universe Pageant, and from 2013 through 2014, worked with the Trump Organization on a Trump Moscow Project.
Guccifer 2.0	Fictitious online persona operated by the GRU that released stolen documents during the 2016 US presidential campaign period.
Internet Research Agency (IRA)	Russian entity based in Saint Peterburg and funded by Concord that engaged in an "active measures" social media campaign to interfere in the 2016 US presidential election.
GRU	Russian Federation's military intelligence agency
WikiLeaks	Organization founded by Julian Assange that posts information online, including data stolen from private, corporate, and US Government entities. Released data stolen by GRU during the 2016 US presidential election.

Printed in the United States
By Bookmasters